The Story of Kew

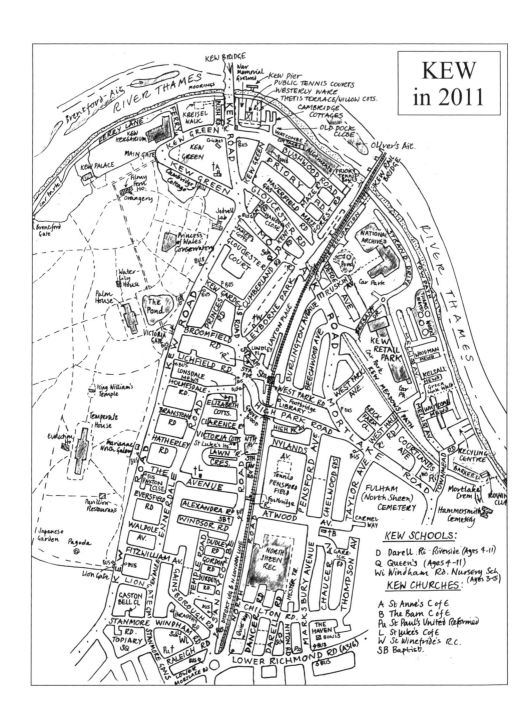

KEW in 2011

The Story of Kew

The Gardens   The Village

The National Archives

David Blomfield

With illustrations by
Anne Abercrombie

Leyborne Publications

5th Edition (enlarged) 2011

Published by Leyborne Publications, 7 Leyborne Park, Kew, Richmond, Surrey TW9 3HB

Text © David Blomfield 1992 and 2011
Illustrations © Anne Abercrombie 1992 and 2011
Map © Francis Brown 2011
5th Edition 2011

ISBN 0 9520515 3 2

Typeset in Times New Roman. Printed in Great Britain by the Russell Press, Nottingham.

MIX
Paper from
responsible sources
FSC® C021423
www.fsc.org

Introduction

This fifth edition of *The Story of Kew* is even larger than its predecessors – and rightly so. Kew itself is still growing. Its houses have spread right along the riverside and it is now the home of not one, but two, major institutions – the grassy acres of the Royal Botanic Gardens being balanced by the imposing mass of the National Archives (formerly the Public Record Office). This book tells the story of these institutions, and of the ancient Surrey village that enjoyed an important and colourful history of its own long before either of them was created.

In most communities it is easy to spot historic milestones: the first move from agriculture to industry; the decay of one industry and the arrival of another; the impact of canals, of trains, of cars. For Kew, however, the milestones have, in one or two respects, been of a less obvious kind. Certainly, like its neighbours, Kew was transformed by rail and by road, but the major local industry has not changed. Kew is still known for growing plants – though of a special kind. Its only other historic industry, however, has now moved on, and that too was of a special kind: for three centuries Kew's prosperity depended almost entirely on royalty. First it was a home for courtiers, then for king-makers, finally for the royal family itself. Uniquely among Surrey villages, as this book shows, Kew has been more regal than rustic, and it retains remarkable buildings from every stage of its history.

As author the book, I am of course responsible for what is included and what has had to be excluded, and also for every claim and conjecture. However, any such history has to be hugely indebted to the work, expertise, and memories of friends. John Cloake, Iris Bolton, Christopher May, Maisie Brown, Raymond Gill have all been unselfishly generous with their own meticulous research. Francis Brown has patiently updated his original map. Aidan Lawes has let me borrow from his history of the Public Record Office. Many other friends have shared their unique memories of Kew. Earlier historians, of course, paved the way – and none more so than that great historian of Kew, the late George Cassidy.

Above all, I am indebted to Anne Abercrombie and Caroline Blomfield. We have decided to keep Anne's delightful drawings just as she first drew them in 1992: several are themselves of historic importance, as they illustrate how scenes have subtly changed over the last nineteen years. Caroline has helped in a hundred various, often unacknowledged, ways – not least in the revision of each new edition. They have both made the book a joy to work on. I hope that readers will enjoy it too.

David Blomfield

The Great Ford

Chapter 1: Tudor Lords (1485-1603)

This history of Kew begins, as Kew itself began, on the river bank.
In mediaeval times the name was spelt in various documents in at least
twenty different ways. It first appears as Cayho, possibly from the Anglo-
Saxon words for a key (quay) and a projecting spur of land. Certainly the
whole of modern Kew projects – it is a peninsula bounded by the Thames
– but where was the original quay? To find that we must go down from
the Green to the towpath via Ferry Lane and walk upriver to the
Brentford Ferry Gate of Kew Gardens.

Until very recently the river here used to be alive with barges, either
serving the docks of Brentford or manoeuvring for space at the entrance
of the Grand Union Canal. The canal is still there, but almost all of that
riverside industry has disappeared – just one or two semi-derelict
buildings can be seen through the trees on the far side of Brentford Ait.
The major focus now is the Waterman's Arts Centre; and above it and
around it there is a wealth of modern housing enjoying a prime view of
the river and the Gardens.

Along this stretch of the river lies the oldest part of Brentford and of
Kew. For centuries there was a ferry here – close to the Brentford Ferry
Gate – and earlier still, a little further upstream, a ford where people once
crossed the Thames on foot: at low tide then the river was only three feet
deep. This is the site of the great ford of Brentford, and most probably of
the original wharf or quay that gave its name to Kew.

The ford was for centuries the lowest point at which men could
regularly cross the Thames on foot, and it was vitally important for any
invader to gain control of it. We know that in 1016 Edmund Ironside
defeated the Danes on the south bank of the ford, and very possibly it was
here that Julius Caesar crossed the Thames back in 54 BC: stakes have
been found sunk in the river bed – similar to those described in his *Gallic
Wars*, with which the Britons tried in vain to hold him back.

There are, however, no signs on land of those great battles, nor any of
the hamlet on the southern bank that must for centuries have catered for
the passing trade. Indeed, it is not until 1313 that it is first mentioned – in
the Manor records. From then on it appears with increasing frequency in
a variety of spellings, until in 1483, under the name of Kayo, it acquired
sufficient importance to be taxable.

The timing is significant. It was in the fourteenth and fifteenth
centuries that royalty began to make its mark on this stretch of the
Thames. First, two miles upriver, King Edward III converted the Shene
manor house into a palace. Next, Henry V, hoping to expiate the sin of
his father's seizure of the crown, added a monastery next door, and a
convent at Syon on the other side of the river. Finally Henry VII rebuilt

1

the palace on a scale surprisingly generous for so niggardly a king, renaming it Richmond after his Yorkshire earldom. The ford by now had been supplemented by a ferry, and trade boomed.

We can still recapture something of the feeling of those mediaeval days if we walk further upriver towards Richmond, and see where Edward and the Henrys chose to build. The walk is worth it for the views alone. There was probably a riverside path even in those days, though it would have been close to river level, and vulnerable to constant flooding; now we are walking along a line of twentieth-century flood defences. Otherwise the river has altered very little.

This section of the river is a joy for bird-watchers. There may perhaps be fewer swans than in the sixteenth century, and far too many Canada geese, but otherwise the birds must be very much the same: the screaming flocks of gulls; the quieter ducks, coots, cormorants and grebes; the herons nesting in the trees or standing solitary like statues on the farther bank. Their heronry has far outlived the convent Henry built beyond them, which was replaced in the sixteenth century by the ducal palace of Syon House, one of many great houses built along the Thames. (In days when the river was the most convenient highway for passengers and builders, big houses, both religious and domestic, were usually built close to the banks.)

On the Surrey bank, Henry V's great Carthusian monastery has entirely disappeared – its lands covered by a golf course and what we know as the Old Deer Park – while all that remains of Richmond's palace, for three centuries a favourite retreat for royalty, is its gateway facing Richmond Green. Before it disappeared, however, the palace had changed Kew for ever; for it is thanks to Richmond that the riverside hamlet caught hold of the hem of history, and found itself unexpectedly endowed with powerful residents, status, even wealth.

It all began with the Tudors. After the Wars of the Roses England's power structure changed. Barons no longer kept to their estates arrogantly waiting for kings to call on them. They had to come to court themselves, and if the court was now to be at Richmond – at least in the summer months – then the courtiers must build their houses conveniently close by. So the courtiers came to Kew.

Kew was certainly convenient. We know that Henry VIII would leave his barge there and complete his journey to his palace by horse, saving himself the much slower river journey around the peninsula of Kew. In 1530 there was this entry in the royal privy purse accounts: '10s. 8d. paid to the King's watermen, for their waiting from York Place to Keyho, with sixteen oars when the King's grace removed from York Place to Richmond.'

It is probable that the barge landed, not at the quay by the ferry, but farther downriver. Until the late nineteenth century there was a creek linking the river to the pond on Kew Green, and in Tudor times the pond very likely acted as a dock for the royal barge – and for others too. Some of the courtiers would have used the same short cut, and decided that this could be a suitable place to build.

First came Henry VII's cousin, Charles Somerset; next the Earls of Devon, one of whom married the king's sister-in-law. Then, when Henry VIII succeeded, his friend Henry Norris moved to Kew, only to be executed later for adultery with Anne Boleyn. For a time his house was taken by the King to house his own daughter, Mary. Henry's sister and her husband Charles Brandon, Duke of Suffolk, also lived in Kew.

Unsurprisingly, on Henry's death Kew seethed with intrigue. The rival dukes of Somerset and Northumberland, who had each in turn owned the same house in Kew, now each in turn became Lord Protector of the young Edward VI, and successive owners of Syon House. Henry Grey, the Suffolks' son-in-law hastily married his daughter Lady Jane Grey to Northumberland's son and plotted with Northumberland to put the young people on the throne when the sickly Edward VI died. They failed, and Lady Jane Grey and her family climbed no higher than the scaffold.

In Elizabeth's reign most of the Kew properties came into the hands of her favourite, Robert Dudley, Earl of Leicester, and it is said that when Elizabeth stayed in Richmond, she and Dudley used to meet close by the river beneath a great elm tree, on 'Queen Elizabeth's Lawn'. Sadly the elm fell in a storm and ended up as a kitchen table in Queen Victoria's Osborne House. The Lawn also fell victim to the march of progress. It is now the Royal Botanic Gardens' car park.

The great houses themselves fell more swiftly. They were not built to last. Few were in Tudor times. Still we do know where they stood. They stood along the river bank and beside the village green – but the green was a different shape from the one we know. Then it was twice its current length and stretched all the way from the pond to the ferry.

In Elizabethan times one of the riverside houses – the one where Norris and Princess Mary had once stayed, and where Dudley lived – hosted Her Majesty in two spectacular ways. The first was in 1560. when Dudley entertained her to a memorable banquet. The shopping list included 'ten sheep, six lambs, six herons, 48 teal, 48 quails, 56 pigeons, 20 capons, 36 coneys, 600 eggs, 41 dozen loaves and 86 lbs of butter'. In addition, there were 26 turkeys, recently introduced from America, and pineapples – possibly the first to be imported to England. The event must have cause a great stir around Kew Green, but sadly the Kew traders missed out: the only local supplier was 'ye baker at Braynford'.

After Dudley left Kew, the house was leased by Sir John Puckering, the Lord Keeper of the Great Seal and Speaker of the House of Commons. In 1594 Sir John thought it might be politic to offer Her Majesty another dinner there. We know nothing of the menu, but, as a contemporary recorded, Puckering found it an expensive business.

'At her first alighting she had a fine fan, with a handle garnished with diamonds. When she was in the middle way, between the garden gate and the house, there came one running towards her with a nosegay in his hands and delivered it with a short, well-penned speech; it had in it a very rich jewel, with many pendants of diamonds, valued at £400 at least.' At dinner, 'to grace his lordship the more, she of herself took from him a salt, a spoon, and a fork of fine agate.'

Few tears should be shed for Sir John's lost cutlery. He knew exactly what he was about. Every bit as mean as Elizabeth, he was also corrupt. Both sovereign and subject knew to the last spoon how much his supper was worth.

In the story of Kew, regrettably, the oleaginous Puckering holds a special place, as does the more romantic figure of Robert Dudley, for it is almost certain that the house they owned was called Kew Farm. It was the house closest to the ferry at that time, and scarcely two hundred yards from the oldest house we now have in Kew, the Dutch House – the building we call Kew Palace.

The Dutch House (Kew Palace)

Chapter 2: Stuart Gentlemen (1603-1714)

The Dutch House was built in 1631. The man who built it, Samuel Fortrey, was a merchant of Flemish parentage, and his wife, Catherine, was a native of Hainault. (Their initials are inscribed above the door.) However, the house most probably acquired its name not from the family's origins but from its Netherlandish style, which was very popular among the Elizabethan merchant class.

Fortrey was a remarkable man in his own right. He was a refugee, born literally half way between his parents' home and the country of his adoption – in the middle of the English Channel. His parents were fleeing Spanish persecution for their Protestant faith. Like so many others who have found sanctuary in Britain, he contributed far more than he took from his adopted country. In his case it was the house he built; for the Dutch House is as remarkable as its builder. While all Kew's other houses of that time have disappeared, destroyed either by the weather or the whims of owners eager to try out the latest fashionable style, the Dutch House has not only survived; it has remained almost unaltered.

It also has preserved something of the age it superseded: beneath the western part of the house there is an undercroft of ribbed brick vaults. This is older than the house itself, and is possibly part of a house owned by Sir Hugh Portman. Hugh Portman was a key figure in the growth of Kew. He is described in a contemporary document as 'the gentleman knighted by her Majesty at Kew'. One wonders what that cost him! Portman was Puckering's son-in-law, and Elizabeth was used to making money out of her visits to Kew. Still, Portman could afford it. At the time he owned most of the riverside land by the ferry.

What Portman did not own however was the other big estate in Kew. This was Kew Park, which faced Kew Farm across the end of the green. We do not know exactly when the big house of Kew Park was built, but it would be described later both as Kew House and as 'the old timber house', which suggests that it was built in Tudor style. By Elizabethan times the estate, and presumably the house, were in the hands of Dr William Awberry, grandfather of John Aubrey, the author of the entertaining, if occasionally unreliable, *Brief Lives*.

Awberry's son sold the estate to Sir Arthur Gorges, a seaman, a poet and a leading member of the new Stuart court set up at Richmond by James I's eldest son, Prince Henry. We know that Henry's sister, the lively Princess Elizabeth, was also living in Kew at that time with a guardian who complained that she was far too lively. Apparently she was always rushing off on unsupervised visits to her favourite brother at Richmond. It is probable that at the time guardian and ward were staying in the third big house, the old Kew Farm. This estate was owned by another Stuart courtier, Robert Carr, Earl of Ancrum, who rebuilt, or possibly replaced, the house.

After Gorges' death, Kew Park was sold to Sir Richard Bennett, son of the Sheriff of London and Middlesex, and – even more importantly – cousin of the Earl of Arlington. (Arlington and Lauderdale, of Ham House, were the final A and L of the CABAL, the group of ministers who ruled Britain under Charles II.)

Bennett left Kew Park to his daughter Dorothy, who had married prudently: her husband, Sir Henry Capel, came from another family close to Charles II. Like most members of his family, Sir Henry preferred gardening to politics, and spent his wealth on beautifying his wife's property in Kew. He invested especially in trees. If he thought that succeeding generations would thank him for his investment, he was right. He was not just planting a few trees. He was setting the scene for Kew Gardens.

We do not know how many trees Capel planted, but we do know about some of them – on good authority. One of Capel's friends was John Evelyn, the great diarist. In 1683, Evelyn admired 'two greene-houses for oranges and myrtils communicating with the roomes below', and thought a 'cupola made with pole work between two elmes at the end of a walk, which being covered by plashing the trees to them ... very pretty'. In 1688, he saw that Sir Henry was 'contriving very high palisadoes of reedes, to shade his oranges in during the summer, and painting those reedes in oil.'

Evelyn said there were 'too many fir-trees in the garden', but J.Gibson in a paper read to the Society of Antiquaries in 1691 reported that 'Sir Henry Capell's ... two Lentiscus trees for which he paid forty pounds are said to be the best in London.' At that price, they should have been.

Capel – the spelling of his name, like most names up to the nineteenth century, was arbitrary – has his place in history, deservedly, but he was not the first great gardener in Kew. By an extraordinary coincidence, over a hundred years before he arrived, there had been another garden here in Kew, created by no less a man than the 'Father of English Botany', William Turner.

In the multiplicity of his talents, Turner was typical of the English Renaissance man. Probably the son of a tanner, he managed to attract the patronage of Lord Wentworth, became a Fellow of Pembroke Hall, Cambridge, and began work on what would be the first English *Herbal*. He also found time to become, along with Bishops Ridley and Latimer, a leading preacher of Reformation.

Presumably it was on the strength of his scientific expertise, as well as his Protestant convictions, that Turner was next appointed the Duke of Somerset's personal physician. Somerset was then at Syon, and Turner

6

was given a house in Kew. Turner lived here for only three years before becoming, very briefly, Dean of Wells, and fleeing abroad during Queen Mary's reign. Still, while he was in Kew, when he was not dancing attendance on his master (somewhat grudgingly, it appears), he established a garden, and spent his spare time 'upon ye sekyng of herbes, and markyng in what places they do grow'.

In his *Herbal* he wrote of the chickpea, 'I have it in my garden at Kew.' We do not know where that garden was, but if any Kew residents find chickpeas growing in their garden they can speculate that perhaps their garden once belonged to the father of English botany.

While Capel's garden grew, so too did Kew. We know from the hearth tax records in 1664 that there were 29 houses and cottages in all, and that only three of the houses were classed as large. (Two of these were the Dutch House, with 26 hearths, and the Capels' house, with 25 hearths.) Most of the cottages were very small, boasting only one hearth apiece, and must have provided chiefly for farm labourers and fishermen.

For centuries fishing was a major business in Kew, and would continue so until the fish were gradually killed off by pollution in the eighteenth and nineteenth centuries. In mediaeval times rights had been granted for at least two fishing weirs off the Kew bank: one was upstream from the creek that fed the pond (the 'westerley weir') and one was downstream. The latter was owned by Merton Priory, and we know that Shene Monastery and the Bishop of Winchester also had fishing rights in Kew. The weirs were made of hurdles set in zig-zag fashion across the river with a small passage left for boats. Documents record bitter arguments up and down the river on over-fishing, and demands that nets of a certain mesh be banned; yet we can gather how profitable the business must have been – and for how long it flourished – when we read that as late as 1809 there were 'ten to twenty salmon taken at a draught' between Richmond and Mortlake.

By 1710 Kew had more than doubled in size. There were some 80 houses around the Green, and many of them now were owned by men of considerable influence. Sir Richard Levett, Lord Mayor of London, had bought the Dutch House from Fortrey's heirs. Sir Charles Eyre, former Governor of the new East India Company's province of Bengal, lived to the west of the Dutch House, probably close to the site of Kew Farm which had at last given way to the development of smaller houses. The great court painter, Sir Peter Lely, had also bought a house in Kew, and passed it on to his son John. This was next door to what we now know as the Herbarium. On the other side of the Green lived Christopher Appleby, a lawyer of the Middle Temple.

In 1710 Kew was still classed as a hamlet; in practice, however, it was now a considerable village. Yet it had no church of its own. Those who wanted to attend divine worship had to travel to Richmond or Brentford.

In 1710, led by John Lely, Eyre and Appleby, twelve residents offered sums ranging from 2 to 20 guineas apiece towards the cost of building a chapel. (Not all of these claimed to be 'gentlemen', and one of them, Thomas Fuller, signed with his mark.) They then petitioned Queen Anne, as Lady of the Manor of Richmond, for permission to build a chapel.

Even in the 1700s planning applications took their time. It was not until 1712 that Queen Anne granted leave 'to erect and build the said Chappell on the south side of Kew Green on an antient Gravell Pit or peice of wast ground adjoyning to the Road there, at this time of no use or advantage to Us.' *Wast ground?* That hardly sounds like our conservation area, but in fairness to Her Majesty it must be said that 'Wast' was then a legal term indicating common land. Perhaps because it was of no use to her the Queen thought that she ought to do more than grant permission. She also gave £100.

This first little chapel – it would be expanded hugely over the years – eventually cost £500. The gallant twelve, backed by the rest of Kew, and by £100 from Lady Capel, raised the balance, and in 1714 the building, with seating for ninety, was opened for worship. Tactfully, it was dedicated to St Anne.

Chapter 3: Georgian Scandals (1714-1765)

Queen Anne died only a few months after St Anne's was completed, thereby escaping involvement in the bizarre teething problems of the little chapel she had helped to found. First, the vicar of Kingston, in whose parish Kew was then situated, refused to appoint a curate unless Kew could guarantee a salary. A further £80 had to be raised. On the strength of this, the Reverend Mr Thomas Fogg was appointed curate.

Then there was a second problem – the curate himself. It soon became obvious that, in addition to other failings, Mr Fogg cared rather more for his horses than he did for his parishioners. This issue split the village. Appleby, Eyre and nine others wrote to the Bishop of Winchester, demanding that Fogg be discharged unless he agreed to reside permanently in Kew, to use the collection for charitable purposes, to catechise the children, to read morning prayer on Wednesdays and Fridays, to ring the bell in good time for services and to stop officiating 'in his Boots and Riding Clothes under the surplice'. In opposition, Lely, Lady Capel and another eight wrote to the Bishop commending Fogg's piety and devotion. The outcome was a draw. Fogg was not sacked. He was, however, told to do all that the Appleby group demanded, with one exception. His Lordship notably made no order on the matter of wearing 'Boots and Riding Clothes' beneath his surplice!

With the arrival of its own chapel, Kew seems to have taken stock of itself, liked what it saw, and settled for a few modest improvements. Gradually the cottages around the Green were bought up and replaced by houses of a distinctive Georgian pattern. This, though, was not unusual. Most villages of the time were assuming a similarly solid, sensible air. They had a lot to be solid and sensible about, as more and more local problems were now left to the local community to solve for themselves.

Local government in Britain at this time approximated – by chance rather than in pursuit of any political philosophy – to the democracy pioneered by the Greeks over two thousand years before. Each man of property was expected to undertake, without reward, a fair share of parish duties. In Britain, this was organised via the Vestry, which was essentially a parochial church council. Therefore, the needs of the established church were included within the overall needs of the community, an arrangement that would eventually lead to conflict and reform.

Kew's Vestry was headed by a Chapelwarden and an Overseer of the Poor. Both were elected by the parishioners. The former chaired the monthly meetings, and the latter was responsible for collecting the poor rate from householders and distributing it as required. The more junior officers, the Constable and Headborough, were charged with controlling the behaviour of persons and animals within the parish. These posts were filled mostly by the middle class, as Kew had a comparatively small working class, which worked in service, or as farmworkers or on the river. It was therefore an interesting mixture of lawyers, publicans, tradesmen and builders that, along with the local clergyman, would effectively be responsible for the administration of Kew throughout the next two centuries.

Queen Anne, like all the later Stuart kings and queens, had spent little time, and less money, in Richmond, but with the Hanoverians royalty returned. It was not, however, King George I himself that settled there, but the new Prince and Princess of Wales, George and Caroline. Nor was it the palace that they chose – it had been mostly dismantled by 1714 – but Richmond Lodge, a fine house with an estate that straddled the border between Richmond and Kew.

Originally built in 1605 as a royal hunting lodge, Richmond Lodge had been leased from Queen Anne by the Duke of Ormonde. The Duke, a distinguished soldier, made considerable changes, but did not have long to enjoy them, as he had to leave the country in 1715 in some hurry, having picked the losing side in the first Jacobite Rebellion. The Lodge was impressive by any standards, but for its new owners it had a special appeal. It lay at a comfortable distance from the King's palace in London – and the one consistent characteristic of the new dynasty would be that the Princes of Wales were invariably at loggerheads with their fathers. The grounds of Richmond Lodge were wedge-shaped, bounded on one side by the river and on the other by Love Lane, the foot road from Kew ferry to Richmond. (The line of Love Lane is now marked by the Holly Walk in the Gardens. It entered Richmond via Kew Foot Road.)

The energetic Princess Caroline had her grounds laid out by Charles Bridgman, and they were decorated with two exotic pavilions – the Hermitage and Merlin's Cave – designed by William Kent, the architect of the Palladian Chiswick House.

The house itself, however, soon proved too small for the Wales' growing family. Instead of extending the house, Caroline decided to rent extra space at the far end of her estate, down by Kew ferry. First she leased the Dutch House from Richard Levett's daughter, to act as a nursery. Later, when her husband came to the throne, she would also lease the Eyres' house, renaming it the Queen's House.

Now the one big estate by Kew Green left in private hands was that of the Capels. Their gardens and the house, then commonly referred to as Kew House, had been left to their great niece Elizabeth, who was married to the Prince of Wales' secretary, Samuel Molyneux.

It was thanks to Molyneux that the first major scientific discovery to be associated with Kew was ironically to be in astronomy rather than botany. Molyneux was an amateur astronomer. He converted part of the house into an observatory, and it was here in 1725 that his friend, the Reverend Dr Bradley, established for the first time a record of the aberration of light. The site of the house and this discovery are now marked on a sundial on the lawns in front of the Dutch House.

We do not know what Molyneux' wife thought of losing half her house to a telescope, but she was not exactly prostrated with grief when her husband died in 1728.

Instead she caused considerable scandal by running away on the day of his death with the doctor who was supposed to be caring for him. Unsurprisingly, the doctor, 'the notorious empiric' Nathaniel St André, was suspected of hastening the death. Unsurprisingly too, Elizabeth and St André thought it wiser to settle elsewhere, and the estate was put on the market. It took two years for Elizabeth to find a buyer, but the wait would prove worth while, for the man who took on the lease would make Kew famous for all time. This was Frederick, Prince of Wales.

Frederick's decision to settle in Kew must have seemed bizarre. His father, the previous Prince of Wales, was now King George II, and he still owned Richmond Lodge. True to family tradition he was not on speaking terms with his son. Perhaps Frederick got some perverse pleasure out of irritating his parents by moving in next door. Also it was perhaps to irritate them further that he patronised their favourite architect, William Kent. Kent gave the old timber house a Palladian makeover, which changed it so radically that it was renamed the White House.

At the same time Frederick set about transforming the image of royalty. George I had had too little grasp of English to attract his subjects' affection. George II was more articulate, but so irascible that he was no more popular. Frederick, however, though brought up in Hanover, cut a very different figure. To everyone's surprise, and to the disdain of

11

smart society, he set out to pursue the life of an English country gentleman.

He used to go for walks in the meadows around Kew, often in the company of James Thomson, a poet whose poem *The Seasons* prefigured the Romantic movement. Thomson lived at the Richmond end of the Kew foot road. Fred was also accompanied by a dog for whose collar Alexander Pope (a near neighbour from Twickenham) wrote his couplet:

'I am his Highness' dog at Kew;
Pray tell me, sir, whose dog are you?'

Frederick enjoyed cricket on Kew Green – as did the villagers: indeed there were complaints in one London paper that the Kew labourers enjoyed it so much that they would not get the harvest in. In 1737 Frederick captained his own team against one led by the Duke of Marlborough, for a stake of £100. (Even then, gambling and sport went hand in hand.) Frederick won.

More significantly, Frederick also enjoyed gardening – perhaps his reason for buying the Capel estate. To give himself more space, he added a further 47½ acres, extending his grounds to the driveway of his father's house. His estate was now also wedge-shaped, alongside that of Richmond Lodge, covering most of the land between Love Lane and the horse road (now Kew Road).

Kent was employed to landscape the new estate, and the prince himself helped with some of the work. There were a chinoiserie summer-house, a House of Confucius, and an India House. There were also plans for a lake and an aqueduct. This was not so very remarkable for the time, as there was intense interest then among landowners in the art of landscape. What was remarkable was that Frederick's enthusiasm did not stop at lakes and follies. He was genuinely, and most unusually, interested in a scientific approach to gardening – in botany itself. He set out to create a garden for exotic specimens.

He found two unexpected allies in his hobby, his own young wife, Augusta, and a nobleman he met over a game of cards one rainy afternoon at the races: John Stuart, Earl of Bute. Between them they had ambitious plans. One visitor in 1750 found Frederick 'directing the plantations of trees [and] exotics with workmen – adviseing & assisting where wee were … told of his contrivances, designs of his improvements in his Gardens'.

Frederick was not to see his contrivances completed. In 1751 he caught cold and died. Two causes were given; each reflected a different side of his personality. Dr Mitchell ascribed his death to 'contracting cold by standing in the wet to see some trees planted'. Horace Walpole, another

12

neighbour with his little Gothic castle at Strawberry Hill, said it proceeded 'from a blow with a tennis ball some years ago'.

Frederick's parents provided a disdainfully inadequate funeral, and Horace Walpole recorded for posterity the famous epitaph:

'Here lies poor Fred,
Who was alive and is dead:
Had it been his father,
I had much rather;
Had it been his brother,
Still better than another;
Had it been his sister,
No one would have missed her;
Had it been the whole generation,
Still better for the nation;
But since it is poor Fred,
Who was alive and is dead,
There's no more to be said.'

The contempt here is more for Fred's family than for Fred, but it is scarcely fair comment on the man who effectively started the Botanic Gardens. Still, contemporaries are seldom fair.

Certainly they were not very fair to Fred's widow. After his death Princess Augusta lived on in the White House, where she continued to pursue her husband's hobby, with the assiduous help of Lord Bute. Unfortunately though, some thought that Bute was too assiduous, and that gardening was not the only hobby that they shared. That might not have mattered if Bute had remained just a gardener, but when George II died and Fred's young son succeeded as George III, Bute was appointed Prime Minister in place of Pitt. The populace – or the popular press at any rate – turned on Bute, and Kew gained a notoriety it did not relish.

By now a number of new houses had sprung up around the Green. Many of them are still there, much admired as prime examples of early Georgian architecture. Bute had not just one, but two, of these. His family house was the one with the porte-cochère opposite the church, but he also owned no.33, which he used for his studies. One pamphlet suggested that Bute worked in no.33 only because it gave easy access to the White House. The pamphlet included a map of the Green, complete with a helpful sketch of the houses. It was headed *A View of Lord Bute's erections at Kew*.

Surprisingly, the eighteenth-century wits were later less exercised over a far juicier story. It was apparently common gossip that just before he came to the throne, George III had had a liaison with a pretty young quakeress, Hannah Lightfoot. There were also rumours that they had been

13

secretly married in St Anne's Chapel in Kew. This was in 1759, only two years before he married, as King George III, Princess Charlotte of Mecklenburg-Strelitz.

Though well known, the story was carefully kept out of the public press. Hannah died in 1765. This, however, was not the end of the matter. Hannah had had children. One of them, named George Rex, lived for a time in Kew, and was much favoured by George III. Then, for some undisclosed reason, he was suddenly packed off to South Africa.

Years later his daughter married a Reverend Charles Bull. Bull came back to England and asked St Anne's if he could see their registers. It was not a tactful question. First, someone broke into Bull's lodgings and burned his papers. Then he was hastily posted off as chaplain to the Falkland Islands for fifteen years.

Bull clearly did not know that St Anne's registers were an embarrassing subject. A number of them had disappeared in 1845, in very strange circumstances. The 'Armada' box in which they were kept was stolen from the church, and was then discovered in the Thames, empty.

It is said that members of the royal family employed the Taylors, the villager bakers, to organise the theft. Certainly the registers have never been seen since. We do not know why they were stolen. It cannot have been to conceal George's marriage to Hannah, as the thieves left the marriage registers of 1759, and no one had entered that marriage in the register anyway. The registers they took covered marriages from 1783 to 1838, baptisms from 1791 to 1845, and burials from 1785 to 1845. What could the royal family have wanted to conceal? We shall probably never know, but it is suggested that the registers might have shown that George Rex fathered a child by one of the princesses.

Some of the story received a fresh airing in 1866 when a Mrs Ryves produced documents in court purporting to show that she was the granddaughter of George III's brother, following his wedding to a commoner. The ceremony had been performed by a Dr Wilmot who, she claimed, had also married George III to Hannah Lightfoot. To support her claim she included documentary evidence of the marriage in St Anne's. These documents were dismissed as forgeries by the Lord Chief Justice. One can see why. Queen Victoria's claim to the throne might have looked a little shaky if her grandfather had been proved a bigamist! Officially the issue was closed. The evidence, however, lives on: the transcript of the trial is kept in the National Archives – ironically in Kew itself.

14

Chapter 4:   Rustic Royals (1765-1820)

Lord Bute's administration was short-lived – he subsequently retired to his own estates to escape his political enemies – but his influence on the new king's character would last the whole of George III's long reign. George had been brought up in seclusion in Kew, absorbing Bute's and Augusta's rustic values. He had also inherited something of his father's tastes. However, where Fred had played the part of the English country gentleman, his son moved even farther down the social scale. He was known as Farmer George.

Throughout his long reign George spent as much time as he could out of London: his favourite estates were those of his childhood, Windsor and Kew. Charlotte, his wife, was delighted. Coming as she did from a small, rather poor, German state, she was happy to see as little as possible of smart London society.

Their country retreat for the first twelve years of the reign was Richmond Lodge. Although he supported his mother and Lord Bute in their development of the Kew gardens, George's personal interest was in landscaping the grounds next door, and the introduction there of cows and sheep. For this he employed the best landscape architect of his day, Capability Brown.

Brown cleared away the follies built by Queen Caroline – tastes had changed over the preceding decades – and created a new open landscape very similar to the one we now have from Twickenham Bridge to the edge of the Gardens. He also designed a Laurel Vale (now the Rhododendron Dell) and added a ha-ha along the riverside, to keep the king's animals from straying.

George specialised in cattle and sheep, and in time inadvertently played a key role in the development of the Australian sheep trade. Eager to improve the standard of wool in Britain, he imported Merino sheep from Spain. His flock was of moderate quality, but a Captain MacArthur bought seven of his rams and three ewes, all but one of which were added to the first flock established in New South Wales.

George also contributed two buildings to the Richmond Lodge estate. For himself, he had Sir William Chambers design the Kew Observatory. Then the Queen's Cottage was built for his family to use for picnics. Both survive.

George's mother was keener on bricks and mortar. For her Kew estate she commissioned a number of buildings from Chambers. The first was the Great Stove hothouse in 1759, 144 feet long. Then came the Orangery, perhaps Chambers' finest building in Kew. Sadly though, it was found to be too dark, and the orange trees were sent off to Kensington Gardens in 1841. The most impressive of Chambers' buildings is the Pagoda, which was completed in 1762. Once it had eighty dragons decorating the corners of the roofs, but they were perhaps too frail for their task. By 1813 they had disappeared. Of the other buildings that remain, Chambers was responsible for the Temples of Aeolus, Arethusa and Bellona, and also for the Ruined Arch, which for a time carried traffic between the gardens and the Kew Road.

As King George's family grew, he made plans to replace Richmond Lodge with something larger, but the plans came to nothing, and in 1772, the year of his mother's death, he moved his family to her Kew estate. The White House became Kew Palace, with the Dutch House acting as the nursery for a third generation of royal children, and here the family would stay for much of every summer until 1802.

As the children grew, more houses around Kew Green were bought for them and their attendants, but domesticity was still the order of the day. Our chief authority for George's family life at this time are the memoirs of the remarkable Mrs Papendiek, who lived for a time in one of the oldest houses on Kew Green, no.77. Her father, Herr Albert, had come from Strelitz as page to Queen Charlotte. His daughter, a contemporary of the princes and princesses, later joined the palace staff as well, and accompanied the family on their journeys to Windsor, London, and back again to Kew. The picture she draws is mostly one of humdrum family life, but behind the domesticity there were more than the average family tensions.

The King was intermittently 'unwell'. He was in fact suffering from porphyria, a rare disease unrecognised at the time, which resulted in spells of madness that terrified his family and unsettled the government of the country. The young princes were also unsettled – mainly by boredom. The eldest, the gifted but unstable Prince of Wales, was soon involved in amorous adventures, promoted rather than restrained by his equerries. Ironically, he was discovered with the actress Mrs Robinson under Queen Elizabeth's elm. History was repeating itself. The King and Queen were not amused, but could do little about their children's morals, especially when the princes broke free and found their way to London.

Mrs Papendiek was a shrewd commentator not only on the royal family, but also on the vigorous social and artistic life that had now sprung up around Kew Green. At that time, wherever kings settled, however rustic their tastes, artists followed in the hope of patronage, and in Kew many of them came from the same background as their royal masters.

She recalls musical evenings attended by Johann Christian Bach (the eighteenth child of the great Johann Sebastian), music master to the royal family. She also met Zoffany, the fashionable court painter, who lived at Strand on the Green. Zoffany was the *enfant terrible* of the artistic set in

The Pagoda

Kew. He famously offered a painting of *The Last Supper* to St Anne's, with one of the Kew vestrymen depicted as Judas! St Anne's turned it down and it now hangs in St Paul's church in Brentford.

On Kew Green itself there were other artists: Jeremiah Meyer, the miniaturist, and Joshua Kirby. Kirby was less talented than Zoffany and Meyer, but in Kew he had influence. He was teacher in perspective to the young Prince of Wales. (His efforts may not have been as wasted as those of other teachers, as George IV's taste in art was one of his few redeeming qualities.) Kirby was also Clerk of Works to the royal family, and was responsible for the first major extension of St Anne's in 1770.

This was at the King's own expense. In 1769, perhaps to acknowledge that Kew was now a royal village, the curacies of Kew and Petersham were detached from Kingston, and became a joint parish. It was then decided that the little chapel, now a church, should be enlarged. Kirby added 140 seats, some in a royal gallery and some in a new north aisle; a new south aisle contained a vestry, a bone store, and a pew keeper's room, later used as a schoolroom.

This last development was grossly overdue. In 1717 a Dame Elizabeth Holford had left £200 to provide religious education in Kew, and Lady Capel in her will had left an endowment to support a charity school. Some efforts had been made to satisfy the terms of those bequests, as there was for a time a school at no.47 Kew Green, then named (perhaps aptly?) Hell House. Kirby himself might well have had some influence on the use of the south aisle. His daughter Sarah Trimmer was then beginning to make a name for herself countrywide as one of the few experts on children's books and education. No one would have known better than she did the extent of the need in Kew.

Kirby was a close friend of Thomas Gainsborough. (Gainsborough's *Joshua Kirby and His Wife* belongs to the National Portrait Gallery.) It was typical of Gainsborough's gift for the unexpected gesture that he decided that he should be buried at Kew, next to the church his friend had redesigned. Gainsborough insisted on a simple slab. In time, however, it has been replaced – it is still simple, but it is now raised and surrounded by a rail. He lies to the right of the west entrance to the church. Round him lie Kirby, Meyer, and Zoffany. Kew is not as grand as Westminster Abbey, but the great painter lies among friends, and within a few yards of no.25 Kew Green, the house he rented for several years from a local waterman, Joseph Hillier.

One of Gainsborough's most delightful portraits is *Miss Haverfield*, now in the Wallace Collection. The subject is known for her charm, but other members of her family, who lived at no.24 Kew Green, are known for the important roles they played in the development of Kew, especially her grandfather who was for years supervisor of part of the King's estate.

Augusta and Lord Bute had ensured the future of the botanic gardens by appointing William Aiton as supervisor in 1759; then George III appointed the great plant collector, Joseph Banks, as unofficial director from 1772. However, at this time scientific activity involved only nine acres of the Kew estate. The rest, along with the Richmond estate, was run by John Haverfield until his death in 1785. It was only then that both gardens were brought under one manager – first William Aiton, and then his son William Townsend Aiton – and people began to speak of Kew Gardens in the plural.

The timing was significant. Since their inception, the two royal estates of Richmond and Kew had been divided not just by family quarrels but also by the old foot road from the ferry – Love Lane. To consolidate his estates George III now offered the Richmond Vestry a bargain they could hardly resist. They desperately needed a new workhouse. He had spare land next to Richmond Park. In 1786, a bill was presented to Parliament that included the closure of Love Lane. It was passed without protest, and the King promptly gave the whole of Hill Common and most of Pesthouse Common (later known as the Queen's Road estate) to Richmond Vestry, and he paid for a new workhouse there for the poor of Richmond and Kew.

This kind of bargain was not so unusual. The King had already improved the horse road (Kew Road) between Richmond and Kew back in 1765, supplying a good surface forty feet wide. This too was in exchange for closing a road – one that had run for years from the ferry along the riverbank to Richmond.

Nor was the lack of protest surprising. The old ferry was no longer so important. The first Kew bridge had been built back in 1759, and most traffic now used the new Kew Road. Admittedly the bridge was rather rickety, being built mostly of wood, but 3000 people had crossed it on the first day, and on some days up to £300 had been taken in tolls. It clearly had a future. By 1786 Robert Tunstall of Brentford (son of the first bridge builder) and John Haverfield II of Kew were already proposing an elegant new structure in stone. If the King wanted to indulge in horse trading, that suited the local businessmen. They travelled by coach and traded goods by carts, and the King clearly knew that they were the ones to be placated. Foot travellers were less important.

The focus for most of this traffic then were the Gardens. They were now open to the public: the Kew Garden on Thursdays and the Richmond Garden on Sundays. There were protests even then over parking, those with the right of herbage objecting to the number of carriages parked on the Green, but there was little action taken. There also were objections then as now to noise, as the general gaiety spilled over on to Brentford Ait, which had its own inn and attracted revellers from up and down the river.

Of greater and more dangerous concern was the prevalence, and impertinence, of highwaymen. Walpole wrote in 1782 that they 'have cut off all communication between villages. It is as dangerous to go to Petersham as it is to Gibraltar.' Walpole may have exaggerated, but the Papendieks certainly were robbed in Mortlake, and they suspected that the coachman was an accessory to the crime. Stocks were built beside St Anne's, and there was a lock-up for criminals below the church itself.

For visitors to Kew, however, there was a compensating *frisson* of interest in the prospect of seeing members of the royal family peering from the windows of Kew Palace, or even walking round the gardens themselves. When well, King George was known for his affable manners, and was a popular figure in the village. Sadly though, he was now increasingly far from well.

In 1807 the attacks were so frequent that he retired to Windsor. By then most of the princes and princesses had moved too – mostly to London, Brighton, and Germany. The White House had been pulled down, and James Wyatt had begun work on the King's designs for an exotic castellated palace on the river front on the site of the Queen's House. This Gothic palace was completed, but never used. It would be totally dismantled in 1828.

Queen Charlotte still came to Kew, but only to stay in the old Dutch House, which had inherited the title of Kew Palace, and it was here in 1818 that she presided over a bizarre but historic double wedding.

She was then on her deathbed. The King was incurably mad, and about to die. The Prince of Wales was married, but had lost his only child. There was a desperate need for legitimate children from his brothers. The Dukes of Cumberland, Sussex and Cambridge were married but as yet had had no heirs. Now in the Queen's drawing room in the little palace were gathered the Archbishop of Canterbury, the Bishop of London, and her two remaining errant sons: Prince William (the future William IV) and Prince Edward. Beside these two portly middle-aged princes stood two rather younger princesses – German, naturally. It was unpromising material, but it was to prove the key to the continuation of the Crown in Britain. From this ceremony – or rather from Edward of Kent and his bride – came Victoria and the longest, most stable, reign in British history, Kew Palace's gift to the nation.

Chapter 5: Victorian Visitors (1820-1869)

The bizarre wedding in Kew Palace effectively marked the end of Kew's brief reign as the rustic retreat of royalty. There would still be princes and princesses living around the Green, but no more kings and queens. George IV and William IV would concern themselves with the village of their youth, and Victoria would picnic at the Queen's Cottage, but none of them used the little palace.

George IV might have been an absentee landlord, but he immediately bought up the land and houses that lay between Kew Palace and Ferry Lane, and he closed the road that had run for centuries across the Green to the ferry. The new boundary to the royal estate stretched from no.47 to Ferry Lane, and included an elaborate new entrance gate, with a lion and unicorn on the gateposts. William IV, thinking this too large an encroachment, pushed the entrance back to its present position, where in 1846 Decimus Burton would create the present Main Gate, while the lion and the unicorn would go off to find their own gates on the Kew Road.

Just inside his new entrance William found a home for one of a pair of buildings designed for Buckingham Palace by John Nash in 1825. (The other would become the Royal swimming pool.) It was modified by Sir Geoffrey Wyatville, who also designed King William's Temple for the Gardens.

More important, though, were the two kings' contributions to the school and church. The school in the aisle of the church had been closed in 1788 to 'reduce expenditure'. Those children whose families were not sent off to the new workhouse in Richmond apparently had to beg pennies to enable them to go to Mrs Trimmer's school in Brentford. Eventually, concerned parishioners, helped by the royal family, established an endowed school in 1810 in a rented house. Then in 1826 they opened a Free (Church of England) School next to Kew Pond. George IV gave £300 and commanded that it be called The King's School. (Since then the name has changed, according to the monarch, back and forth between The King's School and The Queen's School.)

By now the church too needed more space. Kew had attracted new residents, still mostly grouped around the Green. William IV paid for another enlargement, by his favourite architect, Wyatville. This increased the seating capacity to 592, by extending the nave and aisles, and creating a yet more magnificent royal gallery.

Ironically the gallery would scarcely ever be used by royalty. Before the work was finished, the Duke of Cumberland, the only one of Victoria's 'wicked uncles' to have stayed on in Kew, had left to become King of Hanover. (Under Salic law, Victoria could not reign there.)

21

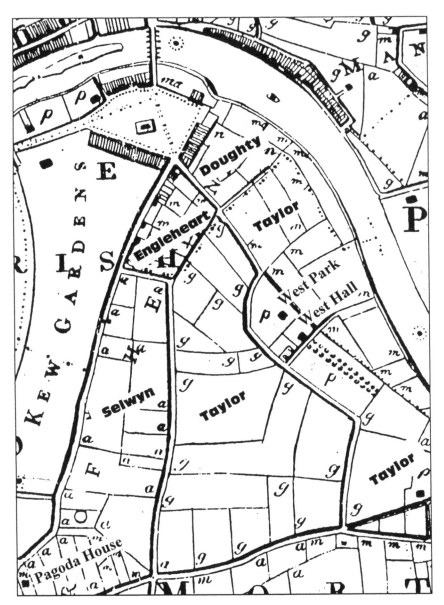

This map, based on Thomas Milne's Land Use map of 1800, indicates the
ownership of the major estates in Kew in the early nineteenth century, and the
use made of the land. Key: a. arable; g. market gardens; m. meadow or pasture;
n. nursery garden; p. paddock or little park

However, his younger brother, the Duke of Cambridge, who had for many years served as Governor-General of Hanover, now returned to settle in Cambridge Cottage (Bute's old house).

Cambridge and his family, especially his massive but ebullient daughter Mary Adelaide, were very popular in Kew and Richmond. The only ones to suffer were the clergy, whose services were punctuated with loud interjections from the eccentric Duke. It might have been less distracting if he had sat in the royal gallery, but he became very deaf and insisted on sitting in the front row. 'Let us pray,' said the vicar. 'By all means,' the Duke would bawl. Then to a prayer for rain, the Duke would respond, 'Amen, but you won't get it till the wind changes.'

One curate was so embarrassed by having to compete with the royal running commentary that he resigned, but at that time some of the Kew clergy were almost as eccentric themselves. Caleb Colton for instance was famous chiefly for spending most of his time in London gambling dens, and living in Soho so as not to have to keep up the character of a clergyman in Kew. He later expanded his activities to France and America, lost his living and blew out his brains in Fontainebleau – thereby establishing our first link with Richmond's twin town!

For Kew, the almost total departure of royalty could have been a disaster. Yet the collapse of this key source of employment does not seem to have caused any acute distress, partly because the Gardens themselves attracted more rather than fewer visitors: visitors were now admitted daily, except on Sundays, from 1pm to 6pm, free of charge, so long as they were respectably dressed.

However, not everyone was pleased. At a parliamentary enquiry in 1838 the supervisor, William Townsend Aiton, was castigated for failure to label the plants and for his meanness in distributing them. He complained that he had too little money to do the job properly. Then, to add to the general dismay, the botanical artist, Francis Bauer, the one man at Kew with an international reputation, died in 1840. The choice was now clear: the Gardens should either be put on a professional footing or be closed. The government took the first option. The Queen handed over ownership, and the state appointed William Hooker as the first Director.

Hooker was not only a scientist; he was also a collector. When he went to Kew, he needed space for his collections, and perhaps for this reason he chose not to settle on the Green. This must have seemed an eccentric decision, for, apart from those around the Green, there was only a handful of houses on the whole of the Kew peninsula. The area was entirely covered with arable land, meadows and market gardens.

All the way along the Kew Road, opposite Kew Gardens, stretched the Selwyn estate, which was mostly arable, and beyond that – towards Mortlake – lay the market gardens of the Taylor estate. Apart from their own Pagoda House, the Selwyns had no building of any size on their estate. The Taylor estate, however, had just changed hands, and had two large houses; one of them was available to let. Built close to the road to Mortlake, it was called Brick Farm. It had previously been occupied by the last of the Miss Taylors. Hooker renamed it 'West Park'. He wrote about it to his son Joseph, then gathering specimens in the Antarctic.

'The house is plain, but perfectly gentlemanly, ample for all of us (54 windows!) with a nice garden & Coach House & Stables, & orchard & paddock & about 7 acres in a nice park-like fence with beautiful & really noble trees. I have besides a noble piece of meadow land which I let off for £50 a year. All this too is completely in the country, yet from Kew bridge we have coaches and omnibuses every quarter of an hour to London for a shilling: & we are within 400 yards of the Thames & opposite Chiswick, the Duke of Devonshire's place.'

Joseph, who was to succeed his father as Director, later recalled life in this old house with a mixture of affection and irritation: 'waiting an hour for an omnibus, or missing it (perhaps both), and in the rain may be! The weary walk from our house to the Church, all in the mud for Mamma, the want of any neighbour who can come and spend an evening hour with my sister, and my own midnight trudges from the omnibus, perhaps from Hammersmith, in case of my own staying at all late in town!'

By happy chance we have another first-hand account of this corner of Kew, recorded a few years before William Hooker moved there. In 1813, Sir Richard Phillips, an energetic and prolific commentator on life along the Thames, took a walk from London to Kew. He recorded all he saw, and commented on even more.

He came along the river. 'As I approached a sequestered mansion and some other buildings which together bear the name of Brick Stables I crossed a corner of the meadow towards an angle formed by a rude inlet of the Thames.' If we look at the tithe maps of that time we can see exactly where he came. It was along Kew Meadows Path. What caught his eye, however, was not Hooker's house. The 'sequestered mansion' was West Hall, which still stands, hardly altered, at the far end of West Hall Road. It was built about 1700, the same time as Brick Farm (West Park). Behind West Hall there were indeed Brick Stables (the site of Brick Farm Close) and we must assume that to Phillips they appeared to form a group including Brick Farm.

Just after leaving West Hall Phillips stopped to talk with 'a colony of the people called gipsies'. He had arrived at what we know as Gipsy Corner, at the entrance of Kew Retail Park. (It was 'Gipsy Corner' on maps from 1865.)

As he moved on towards Kew Green, he could see in the distance the Pagoda and the towers of the unfinished castellated palace, while on his right he spotted the only other substantial building between Mortlake and Kew Green: 'My attention was attracted by the battlements of a new

Gothic building, which I learnt, from the keeper of an adjoining turnpike was called Kew Priory.... Nothing could be so tasteful as a place of indulgence for the luxury of wealth; but it is exposed to the inconvenience of floods from the river, which sometimes cover the entire site to a considerable depth.'

This estate had another more formal entrance that led to the Green through a decorative gateway, just beside the pond. At the time the pond had altered little from the time it was used by Henry's barge. The inlet still lay open beside the school, but the barges now carried coal rather than kings. It was eventually covered over, but the pond is still there, of course, with its ancient equivalent of the modern car wash – a ramp for carters who wished to wash their carts, water their horses, or soak the wooden wheels when the iron rims worked loose.

Kew Pond

Kew Priory and its lands stretched from the pond to what would become the railway, and from the road from Mortlake to the river – apart from a line of riverside meadows, mostly covered with osiers. The title and appearance of the building were distinctly neo-Gothic. It was built in mock mediaeval style, influenced perhaps by Horace Walpole's romantic Strawberry Hill. Its name was similarly romantic, almost ridiculous. Far from being a priory, it was a lady's retreat where no male was permitted, except for the local Roman Catholic priest.

The owner was Elizabeth Doughty, a rich, benevolent lady from Richmond, where she endowed St Elizabeth's church. She also owned substantial property in London. She was an unlikely figure for a pioneer, but that is what she was in Kew. For centuries the village had huddled around the Green. She was the first person to consider building on this adjoining stretch of farmland. Perhaps others had been put off by the flooding which would remain a problem until the present flood defences were erected in the 1960s.

Miss Doughty is long gone and the land that once supported just herself and her servants now houses some two thousand residents. All that reminds us of her reclusive presence are the name of the road that bisects what was once her estate, and the unexpected bend in Forest Road: in her day, her drive bent just like that, and every motorist that has to slow around that corner has cause to remember her.

Hooker left West Park in 1852, and moved closer to his work. His own collections had outgrown the house. The collections went into what is now the Herbarium, and Hooker and his family into no.27 Kew Green, both of which the Queen now handed over to the Gardens. She still kept the Queen's Cottage and its woodland garden.

Hooker now had directly under his control almost the whole of the Gardens as we know them, and the authority to use all of them for scientific purposes. His first major addition was the Palm House. This was built by Decimus Burton and completed in 1848. He then commissioned, also from Burton, the Temperate House, to replace the Great Stove hothouse built by Chambers in 1759. The site of the Great Stove is still marked. The building may have had to go, but the wisteria that covered it survives. It can still be seen, between the Broad Walk and the Princess of Wales Conservatory. It is close to the Maidenhair tree which was itself planted in 1750.

Hooker encouraged visitors. In fact they were now allowed in on every day, and the carriage trade caused traffic jams around the Green. The increase was phenomenal. When Hooker first took over in 1841 the visitor numbers were 9174. By 1846 they were almost 50,000. Then, in 1850, they reached 179,627.

This huge increase was not, however, due simply to Hooker's more generous visiting hours, let alone more parking facilities around the Green; for the new visitors were anything but carriage trade. Many of them were poor people on a rare day out from London, and what brought them to Kew Gardens, and what was changing the pattern of visitors there, was also about to transform the rest of Kew. The railway had reached Richmond.

The first trains appeared in Richmond as early as 1846, and almost immediately they revolutionised the whole of the Richmond riverside. Its boats and cafés became a focus for holiday makers. The impact on Kew was similar, although, as with that of royalty in Tudor times, less immediate and less intense – for good reason. Kew had as yet no railway station of its own.

Some visitors certainly found their way via the Richmond station, and even more via Kew Bridge station when that opened in 1858. By 1865 there were already 500,000 visitors, but even this was nothing compared to what would happen when Kew Gardens station itself opened in 1869.

Chapter 6: Railway Children (1869-1904)

The key to the future development of both the village of Kew and the Royal Botanic Gardens lay in the construction of the Kew Railway bridge – to carry first the London and South Western Railway, and then the District Railway. Now there was no longer a stream of visitors. There was a flood. In 1883 the Gardens attracted 1,244,167; in 1908 the figure would be nearly three million.

It was not as if the Gardens management was making a special effort to attract them. Far from it. When Joseph Hooker succeeded his father in 1865, he not only offended the locals by raising the height of the Kew Road wall by several feet; he also resisted fresh pressure to let visitors in before 1pm. Still, the attractions inside were worth waiting for.

There was the new Temperate House. (It would not be completed till 1899, but the central section was there in the 1860s.) There was the new lake, created where gravel had been excavated for the Temperate House foundations. There was a steepling new flagpole from British Columbia.

Gradually the elegant Georgian houses around the Green began to change their role, becoming tea shops for those visitors using the main gate. However, important though they were, the main gate visitors from Kew Bridge station and the carriage trade were now far outnumbered by those who crowded down from the new Kew Gardens station via a new gate opened in the same year as the railway bridge was built. This was the Cumberland Gate, named either after the Cumberland Arms which stood opposite, or perhaps tactfully after the last Duke of Cumberland. He was also the last King of Hanover, as he had been booted out of his kingdom in 1867. It was not however built on Cumberland's initiative. The man who persuaded the Gardens to build the gate – and who paid for it – came from a different, though no less distinguished, dynasty.

This was J.G.D. Engleheart, the major landowner in that corner of Kew. He was thegreat-grandson of Francis Engleheart (who had come to England as a young man in the wake of the Hanoverians), and of one of two very productive daughters of Thomas Dawney, parish clerk of Kew. Among their descendants, Mary and Anne Dawney would have thirteen artists within the space of four generations.

Mary's daughter married Thomas Richmond the licensee of the Coach and Horses, and four of their descendants would become painters, one of them George Richmond, the most fashionable of the Victorian portrait painters. Anne Dawney's husband, Francis Engleheart, was trained as a plasterer, and among their many descendants were a variety of plasterers, miniaturists, sculptors and engravers. (Several houses in Kew have ceilings plastered and decorated by the Englehearts.) Most of the family were also successful in business, and by the 1860s the Engleheart property covered almost all the land now bounded by Broomfield, Cumberland, Gloucester and Kew Roads.

By then there were already houses and cottages along Kew Road, and it was with further development in mind that J.G.D.Engleheart offered to build the Cumberland Gate. It was a shrewd decision. The first beneficiaries of the railway may have been the Gardens, but in the longer term the ones to make the major killing would be those with land to spare for housing. They were few in number. As can be seen from the map on page 22, almost all the spare land between the new railway and the Gardens was split three ways: to the Engleheart, the Selwyn and the Priory estates. The battle was on to see which could make the most of its assets.

Engleheart seems to have stolen a march on the others. Kew Gardens Road was quickly built up to link the gate to the station, more houses sprang up along the Mortlake Road, and the new Gloucester Road was almost complete by 1878. This was an appropriate name, as the Duke of Gloucester, George III's brother, had once lived in Gloucester House, the only big house in that area. It was now occupied by Mr Neumegen, an aristocratic Portuguese Jew, whose family would run it as a Jewish School up to 1919. It was pulled down in 1928 to make way for Gloucester Court, the first of the Kew Road blocks of flats.

Engleheart might have been the fastest to develop, but of the three estates the development of the Selwyn estate would have the most impact on Kew, as it was by far the biggest of the three. It covered the rest of the land between the Gardens wall and the railway, from Broomfield Road to Richmond. It was at first farmland, then mostly meadows and orchards, or it was until the housing boom hit Kew. Most of it had been acquired by Charles Selwyn MP in the eighteenth century; his estate was then expanded by his heirs to become second only to the royal lands in Richmond.

The Selwyns had spotted the importance of the railway even before Engleheart, and had pushed hard for the station to be sited at the end of what would be the Avenue. They had several houses built in that area in the 1860s, and planned for more. The Gardens also had liked the idea, and had built an entrance opposite the Temperate House.

When the station was built somewhat further north, the Gardens accepted Engleheart's offer to build Cumberland Gate with some relief and prepared to wall off the new entrance by the Temperate House. However, even in the 1860s, community action was up and running in Kew. The Gardens were persuaded by the new residents of the Selwyn estate to leave the view even though the gate was no longer relevant.

Railings remain there to this day, now supplemented by the addition of a gate originally designed by Burton for the river entrance to Kew Palace.

Regardless of the station site, the development of the Selwyn estate went steadily ahead. Houses sprang up like mushrooms all the way from the Selwyns' own Pagoda House to Lichfield Road (named in memory of George Selwyn, Bishop of Lichfield). By 1895, even Pagoda House and its grounds had given way to the development of Pagoda and Selwyn Avenues, and Lichfield Road had been extended to reach Kew Gardens station. Lichfield would lose its title to this stretch – it became Station Parade in 1895 – but the timing was important. In 1889 the Gardens had opened the Victoria Gate, and had achieved along Lichfield Road the grand approach it had sought back in the 1860s.

The last of the three estates to go was Miss Doughty's Priory – or all that was left of it – the house had been much altered since her death. She must have turned in her grave to have it described as a 'gentleman's residence' when it came up for sale in 1875. The land was sold in three lots, and sold again two years later. Only then did the new owners take the obvious step of building roads full of new 'gentlemen's residences'.

The gothic house came down, and the name was for a time attached to a Priory, Maze and Forest Roads were then laid out.

This flurry of building was not the first in the area, as the cottages on the riverside were already up by then, first Willow Cottages in the 1870s, then Thetis Terrace, and Cambridge and Watcombe Cottages. In quixotic disregard of centuries of flooding, they clustered around the osier beds and the Ware that once had been the centre of Kew's fishing industry.

An unexpected observer of late nineteenth-century Kew was Camille Pissarro. For a few months he stayed in a flat at the end of Gloucester Road. He had come to persuade the parents of his son's fiancée that it would not be a disaster for their daughter to marry into the family of the Father of Impressionism. They remained unimpressed, but Pissarro stayed on to paint wonderful views of the Gardens and the Green, most of them now sadly out of sight in private collections.

With the influx of residents the little school by the pond was soon bursting its gothic seams; so in 1888 it was replaced on the same site by a three-storey building with space for 462 children. At the time, it was embarrassingly large, but the managers had been right: within a few years it would be full.

Kew Gardens Station

That the Queen's School was not overfull was thanks to the decision of the church authorities that a new parish was needed to cope with the growth of Kew. In 1876 land in Sandy Lane (Sandycombe Road) was donated for a joint church and school. The church soon moved to the Avenue to become St Luke's Church. Then, the school, called St Luke's Church of England School, moved across the road. These two buildings signalled a radical change in Kew. Kew was no longer a little village huddled around its green. It had grown so large that it needed two centres, two churches, two schools.

In time the station area, which linked the parishes, would become the central shopping area of Kew, but at first it was very slow to grow, and it was not until 1886 that a substantial number of shops was established, significantly with two of the first nine premises being used by estate agents. Perhaps this slow growth was because the Green already had its shops, and the Sandycombe Road had spawned shops in such numbers that it was said that on Saturdays 'people walked on each others' heads'.

Certainly for some time the two communities would remain politically quite distinct. When Kew became part the new Borough of Richmond in 1892, St Luke's parish found itself part of North ward, while St Anne's not only became Kew ward, but also adopted a highly individual approach to elections. An ineffectual Ratepayers Association was transformed into the Kew Union, open to all of its 480 burgesses (voters). The Union not only debated local issues; it chose prospective councillors who were then elected unopposed.

Most of the issues it dealt with still sound familiar to us now: coach (omnibus) parking round the Green; the state of the pond; plans for a purpose-built library. Some issues though were peculiar to their day. Tramlines had been installed along the Kew Road in 1883, and horse trams ran regularly from Kew Bridge to the Orange Tree pub in Richmond. This was clearly useful, but the tramway was badly maintained, and the Union resisted unwelcome proposals for electric trams along the Kew Road. (The first electric tramway in London was opened in 1901, from Kew Bridge to Shepherd's Bush.) The Union also thought the Kew Road was too narrow – it was dangerous and residents were splashed by mud. This problem would be partly tackled in 1917 by pulling down the eighteenth-century cottages in front of Gloucester House, and again in 1929 by the purchase of Descanso House garden and several shops to widen the junction with Mortlake Road. Above all, the Union worried over the fire engine – with good reason. For some time this was kept next to Descanso House, but unfortunately the fireman lived elsewhere; so did the horse. By the time all three got together, it was generally too late!

32

An unexpected subject for debate was the Kew Mortuary. This was sited on Westerly Ware to cater for those drowned in the River Thames, a number of whom were washed up on the Kew bank. The mortuary was officially closed in 1915, but the little room has remained, facing the War Memorial Gardens.

While St Anne's parish was worrying about death by fire and water, St Luke's parish was inadvertently making its first major impact on the future. At that time there was, unsurprisingly, very little industry in Kew. Kew was known for botanic and market gardens, not for workshops. Yet at the turn of the century South Avenue and Station Avenue, our smallest and perhaps our least known roads, were pioneering a world-shattering industrial development.

In 1885 two organic chemists, Charles Cross and Edward Bevan (who had both worked at the Royal Botanic Gardens) became consultants to the paper industry. In 1892 they extracted a substance from cellulose that they called viscose. At that time there was in South Avenue the Zurich Incandescent Light Works run by Charles Stearn. Stearn met Cross and attempted to use his viscose for filaments. The experiment was a failure, but Cross and Stearn found that viscose made good artificial silk, and they set up the Viscose Spinning Syndicate in Station Avenue. In 1904, they sold the business to Courtaulds, who transferred the factory to Coventry, and renamed the material 'Rayon'. Their workshop, recently restored as offices, lay between the railway and the new flats in Blake Mews.

As the century came to a close so did the close connection between Kew and the royal family. In 1897, to mark her diamond jubilee, the Queen handed over the remaining few acres of royal gardens to the public – the Queen's Cottage and its woodland – on the condition that it be kept in the semi-wild state she loved. Then in 1898 the Dutch House was at last given a fitting role. It was opened as a museum, devoted to the life and furniture of George III.

The old queen died in 1901, and the last of Kew's royal dukes, the second Duke of Cambridge, followed her in 1904. His sister, Mary Adelaide, who in 1866 had married His Serene (if undistinguished) Highness, the Duke of Teck, at the smartest wedding ever seen in St Anne's, had also died. However, their daughter May was on her way to become a queen herself, being married to the new Prince of Wales. He would be King George V and she Queen Mary.

When Cambridge died, Edward VII gave Cambridge Cottage to the Gardens – perhaps with a touch of nostalgia. As a young man, when rowing on the river, he had often inadvertently followed the example of his predecessor, Henry VIII, by mooring his skiff at Kew, before walking across the Green to have supper with his cousins at Cambridge Cottage.

Chapter 7: River Traders (1760-1920)

Much of our social history has to be viewed through the eyes of its more privileged members, as they were ones with the education to tell their own tale and the money to ensure that their version of events survived. It is only recently – and rather patchily – that a more balanced picture has begun to emerge, very largely thanks to local and family historians who have used libraries and the internet to put together some picture of the lives of the common man and woman. In the story of Kew this has enabled historians to throw fresh light on the comparatively humble families that traded on the river Thames itself.

The river has always been the key to Kew's prosperity, because for centuries the Thames was the major highway in the land. It brought royalty and their courtiers to Kew. It took the produce of Kew's market gardens downstream, and the dung they needed upstream. Yet Kew has always had its back to the river. There is no line of little – rather smart - houses as in Strand on the Green; no great mansions as in Richmond; no thriving, if smelly, industry as in 19th-century Brentford.

This is partly because those other communities are on outer bends of the river, while Cayho, as 'a quay on a projecting spur of land', is on an inner bend, where for centuries the river used to wash over its meadows, discouraging both industrial and domestic building. It was also because Kew developed into a traditional, almost feudal, village community with all its activities centred on the rich houses that bordered the Green. Once the fishing trade began to decline, very few people from Kew worked on the river, yet those that did so over the 18th and 19th centuries were to prove the most successful and entrepreneurial of the community. These were the boatmen of Kew.

Throughout the 19th century three boatman families dominated the riverside trade: the Laytons, the Humphreys and the Williams. Their family histories had significant characteristics in common – successive generations were ambitious, married wisely, were hungry for education – but there were also striking differences in their backgrounds, the businesses they ran, and their role in the Kew community.

The Laytons were distinctly 'old Kew': from 1700 to 1860 six generations of Laytons were born, educated, and employed around Kew Green; carrying goods and people up and down the river. This had been the traditional trade of boatmen for centuries – the lightermen working with barges and the watermen with wherries – and for centuries they effectively had a monopoly of transport to and from London, which was only lost in the 18th century when the British rediscovered the art of building efficient roads and bridges. The Kew boatmen were immediately affected by the building of Kew Bridge, with two families – one of them that of Solomon Hillier, brother of Gainsborough's landlord – losing business and needing help from the poor rate.

The Laytons, however, survived: they had a niche business carrying coal and plants to the royal family's summer palace at Kew and its botanic garden. In fact, they made so much of their good fortune that they gradually moved out of the river trade and up into the professional middle class, but they did so only after a number of alarums and excursions on the way. These mostly concerned John William Layton, the head of the Kew business from 1820 to 1844, and the first and only boatman to be elected churchwarden of Kew. This was at the peak of his career, in 1831, when he was probably using both of the two boathouses on Kew wharf, just above Kew Bridge.

Problems first arose in 1834, when John William was declared bankrupt, only to recover and advertise himself in 1839 once again as 'Lighterman/coalmerchant (lighterman and wharfinger to the Royal Family)'. Then, 1844, everything went badly wrong. He was again adjudged bankrupt; his house and warehouse, including furniture and coal wagons, were advertised for sale. John William left Kew, and by 1861 he and his wife were reduced to sharing a cottage in Camberwell with a shopkeeper and a milliner. Family tradition holds that he was then living on a remittance from the family. As his cottage was just a few streets away from one of his sons, a 'Solicitor, Attorney and Parliamentary Agent', who employed three servants, perhaps this son paid the 'remittance'. He should have done, as his father had certainly earned help from his family. John William may have overreached himself in business, but he had managed to launch his children on distinctly successful careers. Four of his sons were respectively a bookseller, a solicitor, an accountant and a publisher, while two of the three daughters were teachers of 'French and Dance'.

Only the eldest son, William Stacey Layton, remained in Kew, maintaining his father's coalmerchant business at Kew wharf for a few more years. Unlike his father, William Stacey very seldom attended Kew Vestry. This may have been because he saw no advantage in doing so: his father and grandfather had earned money from the Vestry for various errands and for supplying coals, but by his time this business had ended. It may also be because he disliked the vicar, whom he accused of misappropriating burial fees that belonged to the Vestry. He died in 1854, leaving his wife, Rebecca, to run the business.

Rebecca herself died in 1860. By then however, her sons seem to have been destined, like their uncles, for the professions – which suggests that the family enjoyed better education than that available at Kew's Free school. We cannot be sure of how they were able to achieve this, but there is evidence that the Laytons might have used their royal contacts on Kew Green to good effect. In the 1850s, Princess Mary Adelaide recorded in her diary a visit from Mrs. Layton to thank her 'for getting her son (thanks to George) into the Bluecoat School' This son was the eldest of Rebecca's children, and would later be employed as a teacher at the Bluecoat School (Christ's Hospital). His only surviving brother, Ernest, also went into the professions, becoming a solicitor, before emigrating to New Zealand. There is no record of where Ernest and his uncles were educated, but if George, Duke of Cambridge, helped on this occasion it is possible that he or others of his family might have done something similar for other Layton boys. Even without such help there was ample opportunity for private education on Kew Green. There were local private schools from 1731, with as many as three of them often open at the same time. The wealthy Laytons – William Stacey, according to his grandson, lived in Capel House, one of the largest houses on the Green – could easily have seized the opportunity.

There are some similarities between the Laytons and the Humphreys, who were their contemporaries on the river, though the two families worked in distinctly different fields. The Laytons earned their money from carrying goods and passengers, working from Kew wharf, upstream of the bridge, while the Humphreys earned their money downstream from the bridge, mostly from collecting tolls and from hiring out leisure boats.

In fact, the Humphreys worked mostly midstream, at Oliver's Ait, where Thomas Humphreys collected the tolls due to the City of London's Navigation Committee. He also set up his own business there, initially running a barge. Then from 1832 he and his sons – Henry and William in Strand on the Green, and Thomas William and Richard in Kew – began to move into boat-hiring. Years ahead of their contemporaries, they had spotted the potential of the leisure trade, which was to produce almost a century of profitable business for the hard pressed boatmen of the Thames. The Humphreys' customers initially came from the steamships. When the owner of Kew Bridge applied (successfully) to have a pier on the bridge itself in 1848, it was stated that '1200 or 1300 persons in one day land at the "Strand on the Green" … and have to walk half a mile and cross a tollbridge to the Botanical Gardens.' No doubt many were being tempted to hire the Humphreys boats on the way.

Long before then Thomas had made his mark in the Kew community: he was a prominent member of the Vestry, being Overseer of the Poor in 1828 and turning down the post of Churchwarden in 1832. He probably made a good living, as members of his family would occupy a succession of substantial houses – the Toll House on the towpath, no.88 Kew Green (between Waterloo Place and the Greyhound Inn), and eventually both Park House (no.350 Kew Road) and Park Cottage next door. There are indications that the Humphreys, like the Laytons, were well educated.

Three of Thomas' daughters were schoolteachers, and for many years they and their mother ran a private 'preparatory school' at no.88.

Thomas and his sons apparently had further duties. The City was not only in charge of the tidal Thames until 1857, but also moored the City Barge in Kew, just alongside the Toll House. It seems that the Humphreys were also responsible for the maintenance and crew of the barge, the *Maria Wood*, at least until 1859 when the barge was sold.

Whatever the family's duties, they cannot have been too taxing, as Richard was also working as a coalmerchant from 1840 to 1850, and both brothers took leading roles in the family boat-hiring business. They also played their part in Kew Vestry, as Overseers of the Poor. However, neither of them had sons to succeed them. The 1851 census shows that Richard had three girls, while Thomas William had seven girls and one boy – the boy was not bound apprentice and died young. Richard must have left Kew in the early 1850s – his last appearance at the Vestry was in 1852, and a pencilled note in the Watermen's Company's quarterage ledger implies that he emigrated to Australia – and by 1861 Thomas William had also retired from the river, later to pursue a new career as a house agent and agent for the Sun Fire Office. So Thomas William and Richard were to be the last Humphreys watermen in Kew. They had not run out initiative, but they had run short of sons.

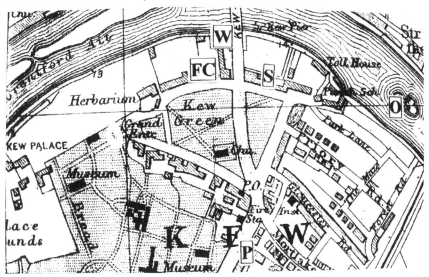

Kew Green in the late 19th century: W̄ Kew Wharf Ō Oliver's Ait
F̄C̄ Flora House and Capel House P̄ Park House and Park Cottage
S̄ The Humphreys school at no.88 Kew Green

The gap left on Kew riverside by the death of Rebecca Layton and the departure of the Humphreys was quickly filled by an even more ambitious family, which was to dominate Kew wharf for the next forty years. This was headed by George Williams of Isleworth, who first appears in the records as a promoter of a 'Kew Royal Regatta' in 1859. It was a fine title that recalled the glory days when royal birthdays were celebrated with similar regattas off the towpath behind Kew Palace. Royalty was long gone, but there were plenty of competitors, and no doubt there was added prestige for those who ran the regatta.

George Williams flourished at Kew wharf, hiring out boats in very large numbers. He also, within three years of his arrival, bound an apprentice, Arthur Iles of Kew, who went on to win the Doggett's Coat and Badge race in 1866 – the very first apprentice to do so from this stretch of the river. George's son, George, also rowed in Doggett's. He did less well than Iles, but as a businessman he did even better than his father. By 1881 this second George Williams had moved into boat-building, and was living in the elegant Flora House on Kew Green, next door to Capel House. All of his sons were apprenticed as watermen. Yet two of the younger sons became signwriters, while another became a organ builder. Apparently there was no room for them in the boat business. This followed a similar decision in the previous generation, where no room had been found for George's twin brothers, one of whom would pursue a less prosperous life in Kew as a decorator, while the other emigrated.

It may be that George and his father lacked confidence in their leisure trade. In 1890, George gave evidence at the enquiry into the building of Richmond's Half-Tide Lock, to the effect that the lock would destroy his business, as his customers would have to pay at the lock, and would hire boats in Richmond instead. He explained that he had 100 boats. 'I have laid out over £3000, and have had to work for it,' he said. It was a huge sum, but there is no evidence that he lost customers as he feared.

In fact, the business remained strong, and by 1901 the family had left Flora House, and were spread amongst the smart modern houses in Gloucester and Bushwood Roads. (See the map on page 37, where 'Park Lane' marks the approximate line of Bushwood Road.) When George's eldest son died in 1901, Frank, the organ builder, returned to run the family business – very successfully: in 1920 Frank registered a fleet of 66 boats, and was living in a big house in Priory Road. His neighbours must have wondered why, with a business that size, Frank Williams did not need every member of the family working there full-time. By then, however, most boatmen were primarily entrepreneurs, and ruthless in employing only those with the skills they needed: unless you could build boats – and perhaps organ-building was useful training – there was no job for you, whatever your family ties.

Chapter 8:   Market Gardeners (1700-1929)

After 1900, the last and biggest estate in Kew began to go the way of the others. (See the map on page 22.) This was the market garden estate that covered the great triangle bounded by the river, the old highway that became the Chertsey Road (A316), and a line along the Sandycombe Road extending straight on to the riverbank. The estate had already sold land to the railways. Now it was to sell nearly all the rest to housing.

This estate historically was part of Mortlake. In mediaeval times its land had been part of the Archbishop of Canterbury's manor of Mortlake. Next it was subsidiary to the manor of Wimbledon. Then in the sixteenth century it became the independent manor of East Sheen and West Hall – 300 acres owned by John Juxon, businessman and baker.

It was probably Juxon's grandson, Thomas, who built the house of West Hall at the end of the 17th century. We know little of those who lived there then, but we do know that most of the land was left first to the Kay family, and that in 1780 it went to a certain Edward Taylor, the son of a Somerset vicar. Whereas the Juxons and Kays seem to have lived in Mortlake or Sheen, the Taylors settled on this part of the estate, but not at West Hall. They lived next door at Brick Farm, the house that Hooker would rename West Park.

Edward Taylor died in 1787, his son in 1788, and the last of his daughters, Elizabeth, in 1837. In 1825 she and her widowed mother had increased their property by buying up certain parts of the estate that had been sold over the years. Apparently they also extended the family house. Certainly it was larger than West Hall by the time Hooker rented it in 1841. By Hooker's day the house and the lands had been inherited by a Major General Edward Leyborne Popham. They had come to him in 1837 by a circuitous route. His grandfather, a Taylor, had married an heiress, Ann Leyborne, and taken her name. Their son, an uncle of Elizabeth Taylor, had done even better by marrying the heiress of the vast Popham estates in Wiltshire and Somerset, and had added on her name. The General was thus awash with names, estates and manors. Perhaps this distracted his attention from his Surrey property, for he clearly paid it little attention.

So much for the owners of the land; its history however does not belong to those who owned it but to those who worked it from 1700 to the 1900s. Perhaps if they had owned it too, its eventual development might have been different. Certainly the profits would have gone into different pockets.

The heroes of the estate were those who leased the land from the Taylors and the Pophams. These were the master market gardeners who

39

worked along the lower reaches of the Thames. Their particular expertise catered for the huge demand for what then were delicacies, and it demanded equally huge supplies of manure for the intensive cultivation of successive crops. The inhabitants of London supplied both. Every night dung barges, piled with the city's night soil, road sweepings and horse manure, would work their way upriver to a wharf at the end of the lane from West Hall. At the same time a line of carts, piled with vegetables, and led by women and children, would be trailing through the night to Covent Garden.

Until the coming of the railways this was the only way to cope with the growing demands of London's ever increasing population. The local arable fields supplied corn, the meadows fattened up cattle (nicknamed 'Welsh beasties') driven in from distant parts, and the market gardens produced the vegetables and fruit. Kew had good meadow and arable land, but the major profits then lay in its market gardens. (Asparagus earned more than ten times the profit of wheat per acre.)

Generally those who farmed the land leased it rather than owned it. It was not that the master gardeners lacked money. Far from it, but apparently they preferred to rent. William Grayson, tenant of Brick Stables and for many years the major farmer in the area, was typical of his kind. In 1832 he was described in the *Gentleman's Magazine* as the 'extraordinary cultivator of asparagus at Mortlake, who has been repeatedly awarded distinguished honours by the Royal Horticultural Society for his delicious luxury'. Grayson certainly was not short of money, but he owned only two of the 152 acres he worked. He was not an easy man to work with. He refused to join the Market Gardeners Association, or to contribute to repairs to the infamous Black Ditch, an open sewer that ran through the Mortlake fields. Fate caught up with him. One dark October night in 1848 he fell into the Ditch himself and was drowned. His son died soon after, and the family business collapsed. Even then fate had not finished its sport with Grayson. On the east side of Sandycombe Road. (part of the Leyborne Popham estate) a row of shops and houses was named after him. The buildings are still there. His name has disappeared.

It is interesting to note that even if they did not invest in the land the more successful market gardeners did settle in some of the big houses. After the estate came into Leyborne Popham hands, West Park was at various times occupied by a scientist (Hooker), a lawyer (Blunt), an industrialist (Doulton), a soldier (Gossett), and a doctor (Beale), but the longest lease, 1886-1908, was taken by the Pouparts, the wealthiest of all the local market gardeners, one of whom gave the land for St Luke's School. In West Hall too, among a number of tenants whose interests lay mostly in the arts, there was another famous family of market gardeners, the Pococks.

The Pouparts and the Pococks had been founding members of the Market Gardeners Association. So was another local market gardener, William Atwood, for many years the Association's secretary and spokesman. He argued urgently with the government over the threat of foreign imports, and the high rates paid by the market gardeners compared to the farmers, but in the long run those were not the greatest threats. What would eventually kill the market gardens were the railways and the increasingly high prices offered by builders all along the river.

The first of the gardens to go for housing were in Barnes, and it was not until 1900 that the Leyborne Pophams agreed to sell their land. By then William Atwood was long gone, and so had his sons who had also farmed this land. The family however had another vital role to play in the story of Kew. Atwood's grandson, Frederick, who lived just beside the new railway in what we know as Leyborne Lodge, was surveyor to the Leyborne Popham estate, and would be responsible for laying out the roads that would supersede the market gardens and determine the shape of twentieth-century development.

The railway had already taken 17 acres, and there had been a line of houses built along the Mortlake Road, until then known as Sand Lane. The next houses appeared in North Road, and in the southern corner of the estate. Streets there were variously named after local celebrities or the other estates of the Leyborne Pophams: Dancer (after one of the asparagus gardeners); Chilton (after the site of the great Popham house of Littlecote); Darrell (after Littlecote's previous owner). When the Council built a school for the new residents, did they knew of the reputation of the man after whom they named it? 'Wild Darrell' not only gambled his estate away; he was even suspected of murder! Fortunately (perhaps aided by a change of spelling) Darell school has defied the omens to gain a national reputation for its teaching.

Atwood chose Leyborne for the name of the house where his family had lived since the 1820s and for the road he created through the surrounding fields – it would contain the Roman Catholic Church of St Winefride. Yet it was not until after the First World War that the Taylors, Pophams and Atwoods were given their own roads.

West Park also had to wait, until 1925 when the crescent of West Park's gardens was developed to be named West Park Avenue, in memory of the avenue of elms and limes that it displaced. West Park house itself went too, but not quite all of it. Among the prefabricated factory sheds behind the houses of West Park Avenue there is a substantial brick building. Its bricks are now painted white, but the outline has not changed: it is the eastern wing of the Taylors' house.

There is however one building in the estate that the Leyborne Pophams left, parts of which can claim to be even older than West Park, older than West Hall, and perhaps even older than Kew Palace.

41

Paradoxically it was one of the last buildings to arrive – and arrive it did, in spectacular style on the backs of lorries.

This is the church of St Philip and All Saints, the Barn Church, in Atwood Avenue. It was created around the beams of a seventeenth-century barn. The beams were brought one by one from Oxted, at the other end of Surrey, and reassembled on the spot. (You can still see the numbers painted on the beams.) The Lambert family gave the beams from their barn, and their Hoare relations supplied the bricks and extra funds. Local residents added refinements.

St Philip and All Saints is the oldest surviving 'barn church' in England, and its beams are very probably ships' timbers from Armada times or even earlier. As such, it is essentially both one of the most modern and also one of the oldest buildings that we have in Kew.

The Barn Church

Chapter 9: Commuter Commoners (1929-2011)

The building of the Barn Church sparked off the last stage in the development of the Leyborne Popham property: the small council estate named after Chaucer, Garrick and Thompson. Geoffrey Chaucer and David Garrick had written and acted in Shene and Richmond in the 14th and 18th centuries, but the radical Councillor William Thompson was a more recent, and perhaps more appropriate, hero. Called 'The People's Champion', he had battled to persuade his fellow councillors to create the nearby Manor Grove Estate, one of the country's first council estates to be developed under the 1890 Housing of the Working Class Act.

A few years later, Brick Stables, that bastion of the Mortlake and Kew market gardens, was abandoned by the last of the master gardeners. By then there was nowhere left to farm. Most of the Leyborne Popham land had gone for houses and roads, and even more for a new industrial estate, owned mostly by Chrysler. The wharf where the dung barges had called each night now led to a sewage works, and all the land by the new Chertsey Road (A316) had been taken over for the new Hammersmith and Fulham cemeteries. (With the vast increase in population, the government had halted the use, and re-use, of church graveyards.) Brick Stables was eventually bought by the Council, along with pieces of the West Hall land, for the erection of Brick Farm Close, and Hawthorn and Magnolia Courts.

Meanwhile the building on the Selwyn estate had also been completed. There had been one minor and one major development. First, Battenburg Road, proving too Germanic a name for the First World War, had been changed to Windsor Road in 1918. Then the last remaining acres in the southern area were developed, also by the Council; and it is thanks to the borough librarian's choice of names that Robert Dudley and Thomas Gainsborough have their own roads.

Oddly the Council had also been responsible for naming the owner-occupied estate of Ruskin and Defoe. The names too are odd. Neither Ruskin nor Defoe was especially involved with Kew. Plans existed for a far bigger estate there down by the river, with roads to be called after other literary worthies, but they were never built. Instead between the wars temporary buildings were constructed for the Ministry of Labour.

These buildings, and the Occupation Road that ran down beside the railway, were requisitioned in the Second World War, and used successively by US troops, who were producing the maps for the invasion of Europe, and by Italian POWs. At the same time, the Green was covered with air raid shelters, warden posts and allotments, and its railings taken for scrap.

Like other villages, Kew was then home to refugee families from all over Europe, and it had its share of bombs. Although most were dropped by chance, as the bombers fled back to Germany, some may have been aimed at the Chrysler factory which now made bomber fuselages. Its close neighbour, West Park Avenue, lost eight houses to one of the first V2 bombs to fall in the UK. Several other roads lost houses too – especially Beechwood Avenue – and, in the Kew Road, Newens Bakery, world famous for its Maids of Honour cakes, was also hit. In all, Kew lost 43 houses, and 29 people lost their lives in raids, two of them refugees, and two American soldiers, Kew's only casualties to V1s (doodle bugs).

After the agonies of war, life returned to the irritations of peacetime, with the Inland Revenue taking over the soldiers' camp at the end of Ruskin Avenue. Then in the 1960s, beyond their buildings, where schoolchildren had once raided the last of the market garden radish fields, the Home Office built an 'experimental' building. The experiment was not a success – apparently the open-plan style jarred, and was too remote from Whitehall – but other developments followed. The most important was the decision to transfer the Public Record Office to Kew. This major national institution arrived in two stages. The first building, nicknamed Fort Ruskin, was opened in 1977, the second in 1996. The history of the PRO (now renamed the National Archives) to Kew is summarised in the Epilogue.

The National Archives straddle the border between the meadowlands of the old village of Kew and the market gardens of Mortlake Heath. Now, these two historic areas, along with the houses of the Selwyn estate, together make up modern Kew, and fairly so, for they include the whole peninsula that celebrates the title of Cayho. Yet, just as the various parts make up the whole of Kew, so does each retain something of its own history, and its own character, and the character persists.

Those living on the former Selwyn estate, between the railway and the Kew Road, have had to cope with fundamental changes since the Second World War. For years it has been the retail heart of Kew, but shoppers no longer 'walk on each others' heads' in Sandycombe Road. Now supermarket car parks and bus passes attract them to Sheen and Richmond, and only the most resilient traders survive. Yet the area has adapted fast to change. The lost shops are used as houses, and the shops around the station balance their books by catering for the visitors to the Gardens. Meanwhile, the industrial buildings around the station have given way to the housing of Layton Place and Blake Mews, while the workshops of Station Avenue where viscose was developed have been given a new lease of life as offices. So too both the great church of St Luke's and its little primary school have adapted to new roles, the former devoting much of its spare space for community use, and the latter being transformed into an Education Centre.

St Luke's House

On the other side of the railway, the old Taylor/Leyborne Popham estate (known as North Sheen from 1890 to 1965) has remained almost exclusively residential. In the original plan all its shops and community buildings, apart from the Barn Church, were kept strictly to the edge, and apart from the significant development of the Kew Retail Park it is still a residential enclave. However, it has almost doubled in size. This is due to the replacement of almost all of the sewage works by the new housing of Kew Riverside, and the insertion of Kew Riverside Park's apartment blocks between the National Archives and the river. To match this growth a new primary school, Kew Riverside, has been built at Townmead. Two road names in particular remind us of major figures in the history of the estate: Bessant Drive by the retail park and Melliss Avenue in Kew Riverside. The Misses Bessant were market gardeners, Grayson's successors at Brick Stables. Melliss was the engineer who designed the sewage works.

The oldest residential area of the village, that around the Green, has happily preserved its Georgian ambience. There have even been some gains over the last century. With the closure of the restaurants along the north side of the Green, the elegant houses have returned to their earlier role as family homes. The church has grown again, but is if anything still more beautiful. The four ancient inns are still there too. The exact dates they opened – and in some cases their original sites – are open to debate, but we do know that the Rose and Crown was active in 1721, the Coach and Horses in 1763, The King's Arms (now Ask) in 1780, and the Greyhound in 1890. The greatest gain is that the towpath now is higher, and the floods that swamped the cottages, and even reached as far as the end of Leyborne Park – in 1928, 1947, 1953, and 1965 – are just bad memories.

The Gardens have witnessed perhaps the greatest recent changes in the whole of Kew. The price of entry has soared, but there are fine new attractions, which include the Princess of Wales Conservatory and the Joseph Banks Building, named after those eighteenth-century pioneers, the much maligned Princess Augusta and the man George III persuaded to act as the first acting director of the Gardens.

The Princess of Wales Conservatory was opened appropriately by Princess Diana, but it was a later royal occasion that reaffirmed even more appropriately Kew's long connection with the royal family. In 1988, Queen Elizabeth II, on her way to open the restored Richmond riverside, used Kew as her royal quay, embarking by boat from Kew Pier, just a few yards from the landing place used by her predecessors Henry VIII and Edward VII. With her visit, modern Cayho was able to celebrate both its name and its historic past in style.

Epilogue: The National Archives

The little village of Kew – it is still among the smallest of London's suburbs – boasts a unique position in the country: it is home to two of the country's most important institutions: not just the Royal Botanic Gardens, but also the National Archives.

The records of the National Archives span more than a thousand years of recorded history, with literally millions of papers, parchments, maps and plans. In addition to government records, census returns, tithe maps, military and naval lists, it holds – and occasionally puts on display – fascinating treasures such as Domesday Book and Magna Carta, Guy Fawkes' confession, along with plans, posters, cartoons, and objects as varied as mediaeval coin dies and samples of nineteenth-century buttons.

The Archives are known for the state secrets they hold – and the annual dramatic release of those secrets that can at last be told – but for most researchers they have a more intimate personal character. Their collection of military records, of wills and maps constitute a treasure trove for those researching family and local history. Largely because of its royal connections, it is especially valuable for those concerned with the local history of Kew. We should use it more.

The National Archives catalogue can be accessed via their website (www.nationalarchives.gov.uk), and some of their records (eg wills) can be downloaded. For those of us who live in Kew, however, it is equally convenient to consult the catalogue on site and then take the opportunity to view the documents themselves. To obtain a reader's ticket takes only a few minutes, so long as you take with you evidence of identity. There is no charge, and the staff are happy to explain how you can find what you want.

The history of the Archives (known previously as the 'Public Record Office') is itself a matter of national pride, as it reaches back to the earliest days of the Norman dynasty. Kings then regarded their records as akin to treasure, to be packed in great chests and transported with the royal baggage trains. (The Archives still have some of these chests, made of pine, plated with iron, with hasps for padlocks, rings at the end for ease of transport and little feet to raise the chest off the damp floors.) Pictograms – not unlike those used internationally now on computer screens – were used to identify classes of documents. Aragon was represented by jousting knights, Gascony by grape-treading, Wales by an archer.

From the twelfth century, however, when the royal headquarters settled down in the cities of London and Westminster, their records settled too. The main record offices were at Westminster Abbey, the Tower of London and, most importantly, in Chancery Lane, at what was called the

Rolls Estate – the records were then kept on parchment rolls which had to be unwound by those consulting them.

Most early users had a business purpose behind their researches. Religious houses came looking for evidence of royal grants missing from their own archives. Landowners needed to trace the descent of a manor or evidence of a transfer of title. William Prynne who took over the office of Keeper of the Records in the Tower at the Restoration found the records there were in 'a deplorable pickle... I have almost been choked with dust of neglected records (interred in their own rubbish for sundry years) in the White Tower, their rust eating out the tops of my gloves with their touch, and their dust rendering me twice a day as black as a Chymney Sweeper.'

Standards clearly improved and when the Public Record Office, founded in 1838, developed its own purpose-built quarters in Chancery Lane between 1852 and 1900, a contemporary described it as the 'stronghold of the Empire', its design breaking new ground in providing a secure fireproof environment for the records.

That site, however, eventually proved quite inadequate for the number of records that needed storage in the twentieth century and of those who wished to consult them. For years the staff struggled to maintain their twin duties of conservation and of service to the public. Then in 1966 a study of likely demand forecast that in 2000 accommodation would be needed for 900 readers a day inspecting 4000 documents. Chancery Lane could never cope. The records must be moved.

Initially Kew was chosen for a satellite office, just for 'modern' documents, most of them post-1782. Work began in 1973, and the new office was completed in 1977. Then it was decided that all the records should be moved there. The buildings therefore cover a span of twenty years, the first block being followed in 1996 by an even larger building to contain the remaining records and offices.

Links with the old Chancery Lane site are preserved at Kew. The ironwork at the main entrance and on the bridge over the twin ponds – home to the Archives' own family of swans – carry a design of mediaeval tally sticks, which were used by officials to record accounts. The slates in the paving and garden wall were formerly fireproof shelves that were installed in the nineteenth-century Chancery Lane repository; the slate itself comes from Valencia Island off the coast of Ireland. The early eighteenth-century lead cisterns on either side of the revolving doors into the building are from houses that once fronted Chancery Lane.

Here the City has come to Kew.

Further Reading on Kew

This list of books and the list of articles on page 50 include those publications generally available in local bookshops or in public libraries. (On the internet, the Richmond Local History Society website www.richmondhistory.org.uk displays, thanks to Bamber Gascoigne, a widget that provides information on the borough's major historical sites. The website gives guidance on membership of the Richmond Local History Society, which can also be found at the Reference Library, Old Town Hall, Whittaker Ave, Richmond TW9 1TP Tel.020 8734 3308.)

Court and Private Life in the time of Queen Charlotte by Mrs C.L.H. Papendiek, Richard Bentley and Son 1887
A Prospect of Richmond by Janet Dunbar, White Lion 1966
Kew as it Was by G.E.Cassidy, Hendon 1982
The Growth of Richmond by John Cloake, Richmond Society 1982
The Market Gardens of Barnes and Mortlake by Maisie Brown, Barnes and Mortlake History Society 1985
The Chapel of St. Anne, Kew Green 1710-1769 by G.E.Cassidy, Richmond Society History Section 1985
The Architectural History of St. Anne's Church by G.E.Cassidy, Richmond Local History Society 1986
The Streets of Richmond and Kew by James Green, Judith Filson, Margaret Watson, Richmond Local History Society 1989
Pissarro in West London by Nicholas Reed, Lilburne Press 1990
Richmond Past by John Cloake, Historical Publications 1991
Railways of Richmond upon Thames by Tim Sherwood, Forge Books 1992
Kew Past by David Blomfield, Phillimore 1994
Kew by Ray Desmond, Harvill 1995
Kew through my Camera Lens by Pat Thomas, privately published 1996
Palaces and Parks of Richmond and Kew by John Cloake, Phillimore 1995/8
Cottages and Common Fields of Richmond and Kew by John Cloake, Phillimore 2002
Personal Memories of life in Kew in the first half of the 20th Century compiled by Ian Hunter, Richmond Local History Society 2005
Kew Palace by Susanne Groom and Lee Prosser, Merrell 2006
Kew at War by David Blomfield and Christopher May, Richmond Local History Society 2009
The Aitons: Gardeners to their Majesties by Frank Pagnamenta, Richmond Local History Society 2009

Articles on Kew, from *Richmond History: The Journal of Richmond Local History Society*. (Recent issues of *Richmond History* are on sale at Kew Bookshop; a complete set is held in Richmond Local Studies Library, The Old Town Hall, Whittaker Avenue, Richmond TW9 1TP.)

1981 The eccentric vicar of Kew, the Rev'd Caleb Colton, by G. E. Cassidy
1982 Fun & Games at Kew in 1809 by G. E. Cassidy
1983 Royal tales from Kew by G. E. Cassidy
1984 Kew Gardens and the public 1841-1941 by Dawn Scott
Extracts from the Kew Church archives by G. E. Cassidy
1985 The first organ at St Anne's Church, Kew by G. E. Cassidy
1986 Miss Haverfield of Kew by Stephen Pasmore
1987 The pew cushions in St Anne's Church, Kew by G. E. Cassidy
Camille Pissarro, an Impressionist at Kew by Stephen Pasmore
1989 The Australian Wool Trade's debt to Kew by Iris Bolton
1991 The Kew Priory by George Speaight
A Kew family of artists [Englehearts and Richmonds] by Iris Bolton
1992 The early history of Kew Observatory by Stewart McLaughlin
1994 Richmond's Maids of Honour by James Green
The Lady Bountiful of Kew by Michael F. Barrett
1995 The Fraudulent Tax Collectors of Kew by Iris Bolton
1996 The Dawn of Darell School by Roger T. Stearn
Alderman Thompson and 'The Richmond Experiment' by George F. Bartle
1999 The Watermen of Kew by David Blomfield
2000 Kent, Chambers and the architectural landscape of Kew by John Moses
2001 Kew in 1801 by Edward Casaubon
The Story of a Kew Street [Haverfield Gardens] by Betty Thomson
2002 The modest champion oarsman from Kew by David Blomfield
2003 How the Public Records came to Kew by Michael Roper
2004 The Centenary of Kew Bridge by Iris Bolton
2005 Kew Pond by Iris Bolton
A brief history of the Kew Guild by F. Nigel Hepper
2006 Kew Shops then and now by Caroline Blomfield
Elizabeth Doughty by Dafydd Evans
The Australian Wool Trade's debt to Kew (con.) by Iris Bolton
2007 Women, children .... and pianos ... first by Philip Harper
The earliest houses in Kew by John Cloake
Aspects of an Edwardian council school by Roger T. Stearn
2008 Kew Road through time by Nigel Hepper